Get Published Business Book

- *Volume 2* -

Why Sharing Your Story Can Change Your Life Both
Professionally and Personally

By

Paul G. Brodie

Get Published Business Book: Why Sharing Your Story Can Change Your Life Both Professionally and Personally

<u>Disclaimer</u>

The following viewpoints in this book are those of Paul Brodie and the co-authors. These views are based on his or her personal experiences.

The intention of this book is to share their stories.

All attempts have been made to verify the information provided by this publication. Neither the author, co-authors, nor the publisher assumes any responsibility for errors, omissions, or contrary interpretations of the subject matter herein.

This book is for entertainment purposes only. The views expressed are those of the author and co-authors alone and should not be taken as expert instruction or commands. The reader is responsible for his or her future action. This book makes no guarantees of future success.

Neither the author, co-authors, nor the publisher assumes any responsibility or liability on the behalf of the purchaser or reader of these materials.

The views expressed are based on personal experiences within the corporate world, education, and everyday life.

This book is dedicated to my mom, Barbara "Mama" Brodie. Without her support and motivation (and incredible cooking) I would literally not be here today.

I am also dedicating this book to our co-authors and every client that I have had the privilege to help grow their business through sharing their story. They have all gone above and beyond with chasing their dreams and I am proud to be able to help in their journey.

Table of Contents

Free Book.. vii

Introduction.. ix

Webinar Invitation xi

Chapter 1 - Three Keys to Help Business Owners and Leaders Play Bigger
Than Their Passion 1

Chapter 2 - Investing in People 5

Chapter 3 - Head of Happiness 8

Chapter 4 - Against the Grain 12

Chapter 5 - Very Quietly the Old Legacy Wall Street is Dying 15

Chapter 6 - Adapting to Digital Marketing 19

Chapter 7 - A Call for New Thinking.. 21

Chapter 8 - Are You as Secure as You Feel? Why You Should Be Intrusion
Testing Your Business Network.. 25

Chapter 9 - From Inspiration to Publication: Expressing My Purpose
Through Writing A Book.. 28

Chapter 10 - Monkey with a Microphone 32

Chapter 11 - The Story of DFW Funny Business 35

Chapter 12 - FUN NET™ 39

Chapter 13 - PMA During COVID-19.. 43

Chapter 14 - Prove Them Wrong.. 46

Chapter 15 - Reduce Overwhelm and Supercharge Your Results 50

Chapter 16 - The Best $100 I've Ever Spent: From Elephant Dung to CEO 54

Chapter 17 - Thriving During Covid-19 57

Chapter 18 - Proud to be a Rotarian 60

Chapter 19 - Serve No Master 63

Chapter 20 - The Art of Not Giving Up 66

Chapter 21 - Invest in Yourself 69

Chapter 22 - "Welcome to the Family" 72

Strategy Session Invitation 75

Contact Information 76

Feedback Request 77

Free Book

I would like to offer you the digital version of my Get Published book. The brand-new second edition of Get Published will only be available on the website for a limited time. Enjoy!

- Go to -

www.GetPublishedSystem.com
and click on the Free Book tab.

Introduction

One of the most powerful tools you can have is by sharing your story. My company, Brodie Consulting helps people share their story through publishing and marketing a book and through hosting a virtual conference, otherwise known as a virtual summit.

Through those avenues, we have built two successful businesses as everyone has a story to share. Your story is most important part of your business and brand and is the foundation of your company.

By reading this book you will learn from 22 people who are sharing their own story. At the end of each chapter you will notice either the website or email address of the co-author. This is an invitation for you to connect and learn more about the co-author and how they help others. I am making it my mission to help as many people as possible share their story because everyone has something wonderful to share with the world.

I hope that you enjoy reading our book and we look forward to helping you share your story.

Sincerely,

Paul G. Brodie

CEO, Brodie Consulting Group

www.GetPublishedSystem.com

Webinar Invitation

There are many ways to share your story.

In these uncertain times, a lot of businesses are pivoting.

One of the ways people are pivoting is by hosting their own virtual conference, otherwise known as virtual summits.

I want to invite you to view an OnDemand webinar with me and my strategic business partner, Ray Brehm.

It is a no-pitch webinar and the main point is to show you how you can generate significant revenue on the front-end and back-end of your summit.

We also show you how hosting your own event can position yourself as the Ellen or Oprah of your industry while building potential long-term relationships with your audience.

In addition, we show you how you can market your summit for free and turn your summit into a digital ATM.

- Go to -
www.TheVirtualSummitSystem.com
to watch the webinar.

In addition, you will receive a complimentary digital copy of my Virtual Summit System book.

Chapter 1

<u>Three Keys to Help Business Owners and Leaders Play Bigger Than Their Passion</u>

By: Phyllis Washington

"Passion got me here and it will take a lot more to keep me here and continue to move me forward!"

Passion is a very strong motivator, which is great because passion is necessary fuel when building a business. Your dream is just the beginning. It's the birthing of that passion, which will ignite the fires within and keep them alive. 2003 was the year I had finally figured out what I wanted to be when I grew up! It was my choice; I chose it. It was not a job I applied for, ya know - the one that feels meant for somebody else. It wasn't a path or position suggested to me in order to achieve growth within a company... I discovered coaching as something fun and interesting in the beginning. As I learned more about it, I was hooked… and it was mine! I've been fighting for it ever since.

In his book Miracle-preneuring, Varun Choraria says, "Entrepreneurship is first about yourself, then the money." Well that's the truth for me and many others.

Here are three critical points that I've learned being a business owner:

- Your craft is only one part of your business

- You must get help… don't try to do everything yourself, even if you think you can.

- Your Mindset is #1!

Your craft is only one part of your business

When I started my business in 2017, I had it in my mind that if I was the best coach I could be, that would be enough to build a

business. I've spent countless hours developing my craft - helping people create what they want in life and business. I help them to play bigger, become more effective leaders and get businesses off the ground. Basically, I help them get out of their own way. Developing people also allowed me to study and grow myself continually in many ways. I threw myself into unique challenges one after the other. I love the process and the results of it all. To me there is nothing better than the backdrop of business for growing yourself. What a ride!

Building a successful business is so much more than your craft. Whatever your expertise, you often have to let go of your focus to grow in other areas of your business. You must develop skills that you don't possess, or you must hire out. Multiple skills are needed to build and run a business effectively. Getting into this uncomfortable space can be overwhelming and downright fearful. It will take courage to go there.

You must get help… don't try to do everything yourself, even if you can.

Some of the main reasons we try to do everything are: lack of funds, lack of time, fear of not being in control, holding too tight to own ideas, fear of change, not wanting to take the time to research, putting on a brave face for the team, just not knowing any better, and more. Bringing other people into the process can add so much more richness for your business, for you and them too! One of the areas that I learned this was with my social media. I fought and fought to stay away from social media because I was so uncomfortable with it. I wasted so much valuable time in building my business, strangling my growth by not stepping to this area. I wanted to use the LinkedIn platform for many months but resisted it. Finally, I let go. An instructor/coach inspired me to move forward. Someone had referred a social media virtual assistant to me. I did the research and hired this expertise. Wow, what a relief it has been! I'm learning more and more about it and my VA is loving it and learning too. I'm now in the LinkedIn space posting regularly. This helps my business as well as her business. We are both getting what we want so it's a win/win! When business leaders try to walk their journey alone, it stifles their business and creates more stress. You can only see one viewpoint and can get stuck in narrow ways of thinking and/or being. Working together forms a community, which is what business is all about… working together for a cause, for the good of each other.

Your Mindset is #1!!!

I'm constantly challenged with the dark cloud of doubt and uncertainty in my mind as a business owner and leader. Questions like, *"Am I doing the right thing or moving in the right direction?"* These thoughts are there so much. I'm learning to embrace this unsettled feeling. I've come to know it as a companion along for the journey as I build. I'm also learning that I don't have to be afraid of fear. It's up to me to master it. Fear can also be a driver toward accomplishing great things! As long as I don't let fear and doubt consume me, I'm doing okay. I can work through it with help, then evaluate my results, actions, and challenges. This will allow me to become aware of where to shift and fine tune if need be.

The biggest difference for me was realizing that I had never built a coaching business before and giving myself grace. You don't know what you don't know, that is, until you go through it and learn it! I had myself on the hook big time thinking that I should have had everything figured out. I learned a concept from my corporate days that stated, it takes two years to really get good at a new job. You

have to give yourself time to learn. You have to give yourself the same courtesy as a business owner.

I'm learning to believe in myself with much more conviction as God brought me to this point and I know and pray that I'll continually be watched over because I'm doing what I've been ordained to do. I trust God, I trust the process, and this is a journey that I'm not walking alone in.

It's important to find ways to continue to strengthen your mindset daily. Something that specifically works for you. Find it and use it!

The road from being a lamb to lioness/lion is well worth the travelling. If you are ready to walk that journey, I'm happy to walk it with you!

READY TO TALK?

Schedule your free Business Strategy Session now!

Use this calendar link:

https://calendly.com/coachphyl/business-strategy-session

Chapter 2

<u>Investing in People</u>

By: Paul Fulks

When talking about my roots, I have to back up to southern Ohio, the location of all my beginnings. I'm thankful to be from a dirt farm.

My father was killed when I was a young man, and my mother pretty much raised my sister and I as a single parent. I learned the value of work. My mother worked double shifts every day. My grandmother stepped in to make sure that we were fed, and we went to the places that we were supposed to be, on time. (Even though that doesn't gel well with my nickname or my fantasy football team - Late Again, I still attempt to be there.)

When I left southern Ohio, I went into the Navy and spent time as a Nuclear Electrician. I learned about submarines, ballistic submarines, and had a lot of chemistry & physics training - things that I thought I would never use again, but I find myself leaning back on daily.

When I actually got out of the Navy, I ended up moving to Waco, Texas. Due to my background, I went to work for M&M Mars, the candy factory. And what a great job! Still family-owned, not traded on the market. They treated their people with huge respect and loved them as though they were part of the family. I actually made the very first strawberry-banana Starburst fruit chew, due to my chemistry background.

It was at that time I started playing country music. There were a bunch of people down around Waco ... Waco, to me, is the heart of country music in the state of Texas. You could go within a 20-mile radius outside of Waco and find more talented musicians than you probably could anywhere in the United States. So, I started playing

music.

My entire family moved from Ohio down to Texas. I got a flavor of the stockyards and decided I wanted to move to Arlington to play at the stockyards. At that time, that's when I started shaping cowboy hats at Sheplers western wear, and I learned that I loved people. There became the investing in people portion because the more people I met, the more I wanted to meet. Everyone's story became something new to me. I wanted to figure out what drove them to get to the point they were at when we crossed paths.

That's when I started with the Chamber of Commerce. I also joined the Young Men for Arlington, which was huge. I have to credit that to my buddy, Barry Sanders. No, he's not the running back from the Detroit Lions, although he resembles him. He became one of my mentors, and led me into various organizations in Arlington, and started showing me that the heart of everything is the person. It's not about what you're selling, it's not about what you're doing. I've tried to tell my people and other people in the Chamber of Commerce, that I don't have any clients. They may have crossed the threshold as a client, but they left a friend. Every time that I do something else for them, we become better friends.

Service is huge. Stick by your word and remember that you're only as good as your employees' word. If you tell me it's going to be done tomorrow, I pass your word on. And if we fail, we both look really bad because no one lived up to the promise. I think my great-great-grandfather is the one that originally taught me that my word is golden, and there's no way to replace that.

I love mentoring my employees. There are a lot of things that I could be doing and make more money, but I get more satisfaction out of

teaching my employees ways to be better people. Not necessarily ways to make more money, because then I wouldn't be a mentor. It's about becoming more intelligent and understanding what it is that makes you happy. That doesn't necessarily mean more money, but the faster you learn what makes you happy and what drives you to go to work every day, the faster you will find success. You don't go to work if you love what you do. Whatever it is that you get up to do every day, if you're happy about being there, you're going to be successful. In the end, that's what it's all about. If you're happy, you're successful!

https://3di-signs.com/

Chapter 3

<u>Head of Happiness</u>

By: Devin Mooneyham

Have you ever gone for a drive somewhere and found yourself lost in your own head for a little bit? Next thing you know you've missed your exit sign and you're not even sure how far out of the way you have already gone or when the next exit will be…

Have you ever lived your life this way?

There are many symptoms of the human experience. Joy, love, excitement, sadness, fear, anger, depression, anxiety, confidence, shame, vulnerability, and a host of many others.

Emotions are a completely normal part of this experience. While they are temporary – to come and go as they please – our interactions can sometimes create certain patterns of behavior.

When we are young, we learn by cause and effect. We are shown that if we engage in certain actions, there is an equal or opposite reaction we come to expect. Some of these patterns we carry with us throughout our life and into adulthood.

Did our parents show us that we should stay the safe path and not take risks? Or base our entire life decisions around choices that will bring security and comfort? What about panic – when you face challenges did anyone come running to save you or did you have to figure it out for yourself?

If you pay close attention, you may become aware of some of these things you learned once and still carry. Regardless of what you may discover, it is possible to reverse and/or grow out of them because our identity is not fixed, it is fluid. We have the ability to create a space for growth, if we choose to do the work. Seems easy enough, right?

The problem lies in our perception. We don't see things as they are, we see things as we are. Which means, growth sometimes requires us to admit there is room for improvement. Some people think there must be something wrong with them *right now* and the shame around that believed truth paralyzes them, keeping them from taking action to grow.

You cannot achieve long lasting success and happiness in any area of your life if you do not learn to let go of the things in your life that no longer serve you. That includes expired belief systems, coping mechanisms, relationships, and even friendships.

Most people subconsciously decide they will fail before they ever give themselves an opportunity to *really* try. All those feelings of not being enough, keep you from proving that you are… Here's the thing – hope is not a strategy. When you decide you want to change your life, hope can only take you so far. It's up to you show up and do the work.

As a health & wellness coach, my job is to be a consistent example of what's possible, but it wasn't always this way. My journey is a long list of trial and errors weaved together to write the manuscript that is my life. If it wasn't for my willingness to get uncomfortable, be vulnerable, and fail forward as I dove headfirst into any new experience towards growth – I would not have been able to create the life I have today.

So how can you start the same process today to put your foot on the gas and land that next big exit away from routine and mediocracy?

Open Your Mind to What's Possible

Give yourself permission to try things you never have before and to like them! So often we confine ourself to this tiny box because it is seemingly comfortable to be identified or associated with specific things, but we have ONE wild & precious life… screw predictability or being safe.

Take Small, Significant, Steps in the Right Direction

Whatever you want to do, it won't happen overnight. You want to be a better person? Take some personality tests to figure out your strengths and harness them, but also be aware of your weaknesses and areas for growth. Own where you are now. You want to live a healthier lifestyle? Choose ONE thing to change and do that until you have mastered it, then pick something else and keep going.

Make Time for Joy

We all do things in this life that we would rather not. That's okay, it breeds discipline and shows commitment. However, you are a magnificent vessel of possibility and you should treat yourself as much. Your happiness is JUST as if not MORE important than the duties you are assigned in your life.

Be a Lifelong Learner

Being a dedicated student in every area of your life will 10x your results immediately. You want better relationships or stronger connections with people? Listen more than you talk. Learning is quite possibly one of the greatest gifts we are given as human beings and in living in 2020 with unlimited resources at our fingertips, ignorance is a choice.

Do not let fear continue you to lead you around, get back in the driver's seat and start rewriting your story now. As long as you are alive, it's not too late.

You are responsible for filling your head with happiness. You are the Head of your happiness.

headofhappinessfamily@gmail.com

Chapter 4

<u>**Against the Grain**</u>

By: Sean Rekemeyer

I have always been one to do things my own way. Somehow, I figure if everyone else is running in one direction seats are already filled where they will end up. That concept gained traction with my Christian faith as the Bible says it is a Narrow Path that leads to salvation and there will be a few who see it. This is of course a paraphrase.

I have witnessed a lot of herd mentality in my career. I see many salespeople come and go in the Insurance Industry. I have been a part of training hundreds of them myself. Many of whom become successful in their careers. But many trainers and agents I see have a motivation to sell first and ask questions later, much later.

Health insurance is a particularly very specified legal contract that has many moving parts and gets utilized on a frequent basis. This makes the creation and utilization exceedingly difficult and potentially treacherous. I have met many individuals and families who have experienced loss due to claim denial and misunderstandings. Some companies hide the negatives about their plans or find a way to train the sales force to miss represent them.

My career has been to go against the grain of misleading, slamming, blindly following bad managers and companies.

I started my career by selling a plan that did things much differently than most companies back 22 years ago. I had to learn quickly after I became a broker of many different products 5 years after that. I learned about the good and bad of plans but also look deeper at the hidden gotcha's.

About 7 years ago, a new law called The Affordable Care Act came to town and the U.S. My industry was rocked and many of the folks I knew left for greener pastures, since it looked like the government was taking over healthcare. I didn't leave or run like other career agents. After much prayer and patience, I realized that there could be an even greater opportunity for my career just around the corner! I did everything I could to get informed and certified to work with the government on this new healthcare platform. It was not easy! There were many pitfalls to overcome like the notorious healthcare.gov website failures that plagued agents across the country. A few thousand strong agents survived, and I was one!

I realized quickly that my clients were not pleased with this new government HMO that only was offered by 1 or 2 companies across the land. I began searching and calling vigorously to find alternatives for my small team and clients at the time. I tried a few options when a new opportunity arrived. The Christian healthshare market opened up to licensed agents for the first time ever! This was like manna from Heaven, I thought. I quickly realized the problems with this market. Strict rules for entry and little usage or experience from doctors made the products difficult to utilize.

After some trial and error, I thankfully found companies who were willing to adapt and create great new products. They combined insurance with healthshare coverage to give the most bang for the buck! And with new partnerships they also created the first permanent individual and group product in the industry because rates are stable year to year! If you read this far then reach out to my office or website to learn more and how I can help customize a plan for you or your company.

I hope this inspires you and this story only gets better with continued input from people like you!

God bless,

Sean Rekemeyer

President of Elite Health Plans

www.EliteHealthPlans.com

Chapter 5

<u>Very Quietly the Old Legacy Wall Street is Dying</u>

By: Corey Callaway

June 2019 will go down in history as a landmark change to the investment industry.

The month Charles Schwab held their annual meeting. Charles Schwab & Company has turned the industry upside down. The change is beneficial to all investors, as well as those who want to be investors.

The industry is undergoing a tremendous change unlike ever before and Schwab is in control of it all, yet nearly the entire investment profession does not understand what has happened.

After the message was delivered at the conference, people were walking shell shocked. Their business model was, and is, broken. The mutual fund industry, the Exchange Traded Fund industry, and the run of the mill brokerage industry models are broken. Destroyed.

Yet, they are not talking about it. The major industry publications are all quiet.

What did Schwab do to cause this? There were two primary actions.

First, they eliminated all transaction fees. What does this mean? The traditional commission transaction business is dead, it is gone. The traditional Broker Dealer does not know it yet.

The elimination of transaction charges on the buy and sell of stocks is a tremendous game changer. It allows for a greater latitude of portfolio management that I will clarify further, shortly.

The second earth shattering move is the ability to buy and sell

fractional shares of stocks. Meaning I can sell you .6557 shares or any fraction of IBM for instance. Or any other stock for no cost. No transaction fees. ZERO!

Fractional share investing will be available the second quarter of 2020, but Schwab will not be first to provide it, Interactive Brokers will.

At first glance you may think "Big Deal?" What is so special about buying fractional shares of stock? Trades have been discounted for so long and most discount brokerages are so cheap, why is free such a big deal? And you may ask, why would I want a fraction of a share of stock?

This change will allow me to provide you an actively managed portfolio with say 500 different stocks. Theoretically, you could invest only $50.00 of your capital, your money, and own all 500 stocks with zero transaction charges.

Currently, I trade my equities at Hilltop Securities and every transaction cost my clients $25.00. I could never operate an account with 500 stocks efficiently with a $25.00 transaction charge.

Multiply $25.00 by 500 stocks (that is $12,500). In that case, I would spend too much of your money and reduce your rate of return.

Now, I will be able to provide to my clients a portfolio that mirrors the S & P 500 Index and any other index, and the portfolio will be actively managed.

I will be moving my client's accounts to TD Ameritrade in the coming months. Why TD Ameritrade? They accept small advisory firms and TD Ameritrade is being purchased by Schwab. That is right, TD Ameritrade stepped up and said they would do everything that Schwab is doing, but they couldn't. TD Ameritrade gave in. TD Ameritrade must have had an agreement in advance with Schwab a

year before the announcement.

Why own an index when you can own something that will perform better and protect you on the downside? We can potentially build individually customized portfolios for everyone.

In addition to mirroring and Index, we will be able to mirror Mutual Fund and Exchange Traded Fund portfolios.

That does not mean we will build that many individual portfolios, but we can.

Also, if you want to create a particular portfolio of companies that are involved in the construction of the Apple Watch when it first came out, we can create that portfolio. In fact, we could create a series of such portfolios that we refer to as Motifs. You could have multiple sleeves of Motifs (multiple portfolios) in one account.

Our world is changing at an exponentially fast pace and we are ready to embrace the change. In fact, we are way ahead of the curve.

Zero cost trading and fractional shares is not on the industry radar. We believe the reason for this is the fact that the majority of the investment advisors do not trade that much. They typically buy and hold and maybe rebalance once in a blue moon. They are passive index investment managers.

Most will tell you that you cannot time the market. Yet, today there will be 4 billion shares of stock traded. Someone is trading, someone is timing. The reality is there are many investors who do not buy and hold.

Regulators stifle advisors and securities brokers to prevent too many

trades. Too many transactions mean too much expense to the client and possible accusations of churning the client's account. Too many trades do not matter anymore.

Most advisors are stuck in the old paradigm of buying and holding. Putting Exchange Traded Funds together and baskets of stocks to try to make investing easy. We now live in a world that is developing uses of artificial intelligence and the ability to dynamically move things around in the marketplace.

The zero-cost trading will allow us to execute more transactions and bring about more Alpha, more positive rates of return, and still give us the ability to adjust to the downside as markets become more adverse.

The conversation I think that should be happening today is what opportunities are available to my clients tomorrow versus what I could do yesterday? What are the dynamics of those possibilities?

At the end of the day, this dramatic change will provide reduced cost to our clients and greater efficiencies in the portfolio management.

My wife says I need to change my tagline to "If you are not trading with Callaway, you are burning money!" I will stick with my old one.

"No business is too small, no check is too large, before you give it away, CALL CALLAWAY" Embrace the change.

Now you have a choice – pay more or contact me!

Corey Callaway

CFS Advisors, LLC

Callaway Financial Services

817-274-4877

corey@callawayfinancial.com

Chapter 6

<u>Adapting to Digital Marketing</u>

By: Bryan Acosta

During this pandemic, many business owners have had to adapt to digital and have become more open to Digital Marketing. Digital marketing hasn't been around as long as traditional marketing, but it's been long enough that we know how effective it is. At Advent Trinity, we often get the question, "What exactly is digital marketing?"

The simple answer is— it's just marketing.

Digital marketing is just another platform to spread the word about your business. In fact, you will get results that you just can't get from traditional marketing (i.e.: Radio/TV spots, newspaper advertising, billboards, direct mailing).

So, what is digital marketing and how does it work?

Digital Marketing Defined

Digital marketing is the act of promoting and selling products and services by leveraging online marketing tactics through social media, search engines, and email. Basically, anything you can do online to reach customers.

These days, everyone is hanging out online, and you need to be there, too.

How Digital Marketing Works

Digital marketing works by creating points of interaction on a variety of digital channels, like Facebook, search engines, email, and YouTube, to build a relationship with prospects. This helps you create familiarity and trust with your prospective clients.

With digital marketing, you can actually become a guide and a trusted friend—so when you make a recommendation, people are eager to listen (and buy).

The Key to Digital Marketing Success

You need to have a strategy to take customers seamlessly on a journey from awareness to engagement to conversion and beyond.

Digital marketing makes marketing easier, faster, and more effective than other forms of marketing. It gives you multiple channels where you can connect with people and you can immediately follow analytics to see if your tactic is working.

However, don't randomly adopt digital tactics or focus exclusively on a single one. It's important to have variety and engage your potential customer in several ways.

Digital marketing shortens the journey from strangers to buyers and boosts the lifetime value of every customer. It gives consumers options, and in turn, you can customize your customer's experience.

During this pandemic, we have been helping many businesses go digital with Web Design, SEO, and Social Media Marketing. We have even built mobile apps. If you are serious about transforming your business to go digital visit our website.

www.AdventTrinity.com

Chapter 7

<u>A Call for New Thinking</u>

By: Daniel Pope

Believe or not, I struggle with being "**too loud**". I'm just an extrovert with passion that loves life and love to encourage others. Perhaps I am an acquired taste, but show me some grace, I might grow on you. I'm really humble at heart with the passion and empathy that truly care for people. **I am primarily a right brain thinker**. I have a unique skill set as do you. Our daily challenge is knowing how to best apply our skills, experience, in a way that brings expertise to our business, value to our customer and meaningful relationships in business and life.

In today's business world a powerful force is emerging that is challenging the way we do business. This way wave of change was in play even before this present pandemic. This dynamic is forcing fundamental change to our typical left brain, analytic, methodical approach to business. **Let me explain.**

For last three hundred plus years we have transitioned from the Agricultural Age of the **farmer**, to the Industrial Age of the **factory worker,** into the Information Age (late 19th century-20th century) of the **knowledge worker.** Then beginning in the late 1990's another transition began to take root that is fueled by rapidly increasing digital technology and the explosive use of the internet. This very conceptual, visionary, illustrative dynamic force is causing the business world to a shift beyond a core of mere facts and information to succeed. What is becoming highly valued is a more "right brain" directed business approach that calls for development and an appreciation skill that will be essential to possess if one is to thrive and succeed in the new present.

This new conceptual age is the product of our prior successes and the technologies of our making which have resulted in **affluence** and **personal abundance, powerful technologies** and **globalization** says Author Dan Pink in his book *"A Whole New Mind; Why Right Brainers Will Rule the Future"*. Think of how this new conceptual approach is driving change. Everyone has access to more information than we could ever hope to use, right at our fingertips. The future is not in how much you know. The old school way of knowing more for business advantage is behind us. The future is about how you use that information. It is a more imaginative, even counter intuitive approach to how we do business! This change is causing us to acquire a <u>sense of empathy</u> , recognize the power of beauty, discover meaning from inherently neutral objects or ideas. It is compelling us to be more adept at storytelling and using narrative to communicate. These are skills and tasks that only we can accomplish, of which **NO** machine or program has accurately managed to do consistently.

Higher order thinking and creative problem-solving are the new in-demand skills in the 21st century, and they rely on our ability to find meaning, to see things that exist outside of raw facts and numbers, to see the beauty and identify meaning in patterns and creatively use our insights to solve problems that cross a variety of different fields.

It is the discovery that values a "High Concept, High Touch" approach to business. What I am finding with great delight is that my "right" brain "R-Directed" thinking is more appreciated, needed, and validated in the conceptual age.

My challenge is to properly channel my passion, correctly apply my skill sets, and continually improve my EQ (social business skills) to succeed and thrive.

Dan's book shared a road map for success using "Six Senses" needed to develop and cultivate success in this conceptual culture. Let me briefly share their relevance and then encourage you see how they might apply in your business.

1. **DESIGN**- In this age of excess, affluence and plethora of choices, **we need to go beyond offering what is merely functional.** Customers want beauty, whimsy, creativity, and emotional appeal in the products we deliver and the services we offer. They want more than just customer service, they want an "experience" even a small one.

2. **STORY** -We need to communication that is more narrative driven. Story does not replace analytical thinking, it supplements it. Storytelling skills need to be part of our business toolboxes. Story expresses our knowledge more effectively and to a wider audience. Science confirms that the human brain is wired for story. We consume and communicate in story all day. We need realize that our receiver's heart/mind is asking one central question, **"Give me a reason to care."** If you want your story to stick and be remembered it must contain a measure of emotion.

3. **Symphony**- is largely about the need to develop the skill to create some understanding and connection between the diverse life disciplines that seem disconnected. It the skill of using analogy and seeing one thing in terms of another. **Symphony sees the big picture, like a conductor sees the orchestra, and skillfully blends the diverse instruments together to make beautiful music we all enjoy and benefit from.**

4. **Empathy**- This vital skill is the ability to imagine one's self in someone else's position and to intuitively feel their feelings. **It requires attuning yourself to the other person.** It goes beyond the capacity of mere logic. Empathy calls for forging relationships of trust and authenticity with the goal of inspiring and empowering others.

5. **Play**-the skill of giving yourself permission to go beyond a life that unbalanced by constant business seriousness. **Many companies today see the importance of helping workers achieve a better life-work balance.** They realize that this balance leads to more productive, healthier, happy employees.

6. **Meaning**- This last skill correctly understands the truth **that it is not the accumulation of stuff that really makes a person happy or measures success.** Many a person has raced down the business road, greedily climbing the ladder of "success" only to get to end of their career and realize they had placed their ladder against the wrong building. They look down and see broken relationships and loss of real meaningful life purpose. They have taken so much and given back very little. We were created to want to be a part of something greater than ourselves. There is great personal power in giving back, serving those in need and paying it forward; that my friend is true long-lasting success!

I would encourage you to read Dan's book; **A Whole New Mind.** Much of what I have shared, and the foundation of my success can be traced to what I learned from this book. Check out my website at -

www.roaringgoodphotography.com for free resources to help your business.

Chapter 8

<u>Are You as Secure as You Feel?</u>
<u>Why You Should Be Intrusion Testing Your Business Network</u>

By: Robert Blake

As a business owner, you have a vested interest in the security of your network and the integrity of the data it contains. Even a small data loss could mean months of painstaking recovery, and a large data breach could put your firm out of business for good.

Knowing that the security of your data is one of your key responsibilities as a business owner, you have to do everything you can to lock down systems and protect the data on your network. You keep your servers updated and you follow best practices with your desktops and mobile devices. But are you really as secure as you feel?

If you have not done formal intrusion testing on your business network, you could be relying on blind faith and misplaced confidence. Without a formal plan to probe your network for weaknesses, you could be setting yourself up for some very unpleasant surprises. Here are some reasons why intrusion testing is necessary for every business owner:

Intrusion Testing is about Uncovering Hidden Weaknesses

No matter how secure you think your network is, there may be weaknesses hiding in plain sight. From custom software to old accounts that are still active, each one of these weaknesses presents an entryway into your network.

The companies that conduct intrusion detection testing are experts at finding hidden weaknesses. They make your business network more secure with every back door they close. Relying on them instead of

your own limited knowledge will help you find the dangers you didn't even know were there.

Intrusion Testing Will Help You Prepare for Emerging Threats

The cyber security landscape is always changing, and the bad guys are constantly adapting their methods and fine tuning their nefarious plans. Armed with an in-depth knowledge of what works and what doesn't, they change their tactics and work hard to overcome the cyber defenses business owners have built.

No matter how good you are at running your business, chances are you are not a cyber security expert. By outsourcing this key part of your cyber defenses, you gain access to real expertise, including detecting emerging threats.

If you want to keep your business network secure, it is not enough to protect yourself against known threats. Identifying and responding to new threats as they emerge is even more crucial.

Intrusion Detecting Can Help Your Business Stay Compliant

For businesses in some industries, regular intrusion testing is more than a good idea - it is a regulatory requirement. From pharmaceutical makers and health insurance companies to banks and brokerage firms, many businesses are required to continuously monitor their networks for threats.

Failing to take these threats seriously and respond to them in real time could trigger civil penalties, fines and other serious consequences. By conducting regular intrusion testing, firms in those key industries can protect themselves, their customers, and the reputations they have worked so hard to build.

Intrusion testing is a key part of keeping your network secure, and one you cannot afford to ignore. If you have not yet conducted intrusion testing on your network, your data may not be as secure as you think it is. It's time to act.

Bit by Bit Computer Consultants

721 North Fielder Suite B, Arlington TX 76012

www.bitxbit.com/texas

877-560-5831 #190

Chapter 9

From Inspiration to Publication: Expressing My Purpose Through Writing A Book

By: Jennifer McSween

Inspired by a Book

In 2013, I began writing a book I had been inspired write 11 years earlier. I struggled for 4 years with no results. I remembered the exact moment I received the inspiration.

At the time, I remember feeling compelled to write this book. I not only felt certain I could do it, but that it was something I needed to do.

Getting the Inspiration

I was in a Wisconsin airport during a 3-hour wait for a connecting flight home to Montreal. I was returning from *Pathways of Light* spiritual college in Kiel, Wisconsin. I had attended the In-Person Training section of my spiritual counselor training program.

The day before, August 10th, we became Ordained. We had completed our training and were now Certified Ordained Ministerial Counselors. We were to serve as *"Inner"* Guidance Counselors of sorts. Our role would be to help people connect with the wisdom within themselves. This would allow them to heal those areas of their lives with which they were not at peace.

One of the gifts we received at our ordination was a book titled *"Inner Healing"* by Dan Joseph. I began reading that book while waiting for my flight. Dan wrote in a very clear, simple and engaging manner, and I found myself drawn in from the beginning. In the book, he shared a 3-step process he had developed for finding peace whenever he felt troubled.

Dan's process was practical, so I tried applying it right away on a minor troubling situation that came to mind. I immediately felt a bit less troubled. I found Dan's process not only simple and practical, but very effective.

I found myself thinking that I would love to write a similar book to share simple, practical, spiritual processes. The more I thought about it, the greater the desire and confidence I felt I *could* do it!

As I entertained the idea, I became more and more excited. I had come to believe that my purpose was to help people heal and transform their lives. Writing a book would be yet another way to express my purpose!

I knew then, without a doubt, I would one day be helping people heal and transform through my own book.

Losing Momentum

Over the next few years, my focus was on studying and learning the teachings, *A Course in Miracles*. I built a *Course in Miracles* based counselling practice. I taught classes and workshops at a local spiritual college. I spoke about it at spiritual Centers and Conferences.

The thought of writing a book never left my mind, but I no longer felt as certain that I could. I was doubting my ability. And in spite of my ongoing studies and practice of my subject, I doubted my credibility.

I had lost the vision of why I wanted to write in the first place and no longer felt inspired.

This was my state of mind when I attempted to write my book in 2013. For 4 years I struggled with imposter syndrome. I struggled to

get the information out of my head and onto the pages.

So, I let it go.

On March 10th, 2017, I started writing my book again from scratch and completed my first rough draft in 27 days. I published that book *"True Forgiveness: The Proven Path from Pain to Power In 5 Simple Steps"* October of 2017.

The entire journey from blank page to hitting Publish was effortless and felt guided. This time my sole focus was on expressing my purpose in the form of a book.

I was very excited!

During the time I was writing, there was not one day I woke up *not* wanting to write. And there was this constant underlying feeling of joy.

When I paid an Editor $300.00 and got back something I couldn't use, I was led to an Editor who knew my material better than I did. A non-fiction writer's dream, right?

At the last minute I decided to have a Foreword written after all, I asked Revs. Robert and Mary Stoelting. They are the founders of *Pathways of Light* Spiritual College. It was they who gifted me the book *"Inner Healing"* the book that inspired me to write a book of my own.

They agreed and wrote the beautiful Foreword for *True Forgiveness*.

What Changed

In 2016, I healed a painful situation with which I struggled throughout my life. My method of healing was *"True Forgiveness"*, the process I shared in my book of the same title.

Practicing *True Forgiveness* allowed me to let go of the doubts and fears that kept me from writing. I felt inspired and capable again. So, I acted on that inspiration and kept on taking action following through to completion.

www.RevJenniferMcSween.com

Chapter 10

<u>Monkey with a Microphone</u>

By: Bryan Weatherford

Public Speaking is one of the top fears of most people. While I certainly have my own fears, public speaking is not one of them. I've been a talker as far back as I can remember. I was never a Debate or Thespian kind of guy in school, but I certainly made my share of presentations, and speeches. I've always had a knack for talking to people. One-on-one, small groups, or large audiences, I learned early on that the first rule of being a good speaker is to be a great listener.

Looking back, my life as a "professional speaker" began with my very first job. I was a telephone solicitor for Hilltop Lake Resorts, in beautiful Bridgeport Texas. Cold calling people to set appointments for prospects to get pitched to purchase land near "the giant Texas Shaped Swimming Pool", while not a glorious position, certainly paid well. In a time when the minimum wage in Texas was $1.70 per hour, I was a 15-year old kid making $10 per hour. Not bad I'd say.

Shortly after that, I began my journey in the Hospitality/Attraction industry. With stints at Six Flags over Texas, Putt-Putt Golf Courses, Wet'n Wild, and Busch Entertainment Corporation. I found my niche "selling fun". I learned the key to sales is: 1) Belief in yourself and 2) Belief in your product. I always enjoyed meeting with people and offering them discount admission ticket programs for their staff and guests, or better yet, booking their employee outings. I had multiple opportunities to sell everything from insurance to copiers, from cars to houses. Let's face it though, not everyone needs a new copier, but who doesn't need a little fun in their life?

While working in the theme park industry, I became involved with numerous non-profit groups. I helped them book the venue for their

events, served on their Board of Directors, and spread the word about their organization and their events. I was hooked. I later started All In Promotions. In addition to selling promotional products through this company, I used my speaking skills again as an emcee and an auctioneer for charity events. We've all attended Black-Tie Galas that include live auctions. Many times, these events bring in "real" auctioneers for their live auctions. While their patter is impressive, it flat out doesn't work. Attendees of these events don't buy cows for a living. Because of this, they are intimidated, afraid to scratch their nose for fear of bidding on a trip to Cabo they can't afford, and don't bid on anything.

My take is different. I'm not a Fast-Talking-Cow-Selling Auctioneer. I'm more of a wannabe comedian. I joke with the audience, play bidders off of each other, keep everyone at ease, and raise money for the organization. A lot of money. To date, I have helped groups raise more than 4-million dollars through live auctions alone. As I like to say, "I'm not the guy who can write the big check, but I am the guy who can get the people who write the big checks to write bigger checks. I call it my Spiritual Gift of Gab.

Throughout my life, I have been blessed to have what I refer to as "Forest Gump Moments". Out of nowhere, opportunities just pop into my life. Because of my longtime obsession with poker, I landed a spot on a statewide TV Commercial for the Texas Lottery Commission as a poker dealer. Next up, while working for Alley Cats Entertainment, I was on a segment of Storage Wars Texas. Somehow my experience as a former Professional Putt-Putt Player made me the perfect "expert" to assess the value of a practice putting green found inside a storage unit purchased by the show hosts. I don't know about all that, but it sure was fun.

My favorite such moment is landing a job as a TV talk show host. I have helped over 1000 guests share their stories on my show, All In with Bryan Weatherford on BIZTV. I was a frequent guest on the show. When the host took a new job elsewhere, ownership offered me the position and I haven't looked back. My show now airs in DFW, Austin, and Los Angeles.

As my pastor likes to say:

"Every person has a name. Every name has a story. And every story matters to God."

bryan@biztvtx.com

817-917-3440

Chapter 11

<u>The Story of DFW Funny Business</u>

By: Margaret Clauder

In 1989, Margaret Clauder was working for Ortho Pharmaceutical (a division of Johnson & Johnson) as a pharmaceutical sales representative. Her first son, John, was cared for during the day at a childcare center in Grand Prairie, Texas. She and her husband, Mark, took turns picking up John from his daycare center. On a warm spring day in 1989, Margaret was in the kitchen preparing dinner after work. It was Mark's turn to pick up John on his way home from his job. The center normally closed at 6:30 PM and sometimes he cut it a little close in picking up John before late charges started kicking in. On this particular day, Mark arrived at the daycare center at 6:25 PM. It was already closed. The front door was locked tight and all the lights were out. Mark figured he and Margaret had gotten their wires crossed regarding whose turn it was to pick up John (it had happened before). Obviously, Margaret had picked up the boy on her way home from work. Mark headed home.

Upon entering the kitchen through the garage, Margaret looked at her husband and questioned "Where's John?" To which Mark responded, "Didn't YOU pick him up from the daycare?" "No, it's your day to do it" replied Margaret. Dread spread through both parents as they realized their precious 4-year-old was missing. Neither parent had picked up the child. Mark headed back to the daycare to double check the doors and to look into the windows of every classroom.

Meanwhile, Margaret began to frantically call anyone she could think of to get in touch with the daycare director. She was finally able to track her down to an exercise class she was taking at the time. She was pulled out of her class and headed to the daycare to open the

door. Meanwhile, Mark was up at the daycare looking in all the windows. All the classrooms were empty. One classroom had the blinds down and the room was dark inside. Could that be John's classroom? Was he still inside?

Back home, Margaret stood next to the phone awaiting any word. This was before cell phones were in use. Mark would have to call her via a land line or go back to the house to let her know what was going on. She called the police and explained the situation. They sprang into action and went straight to the daycare. The police arrived before the director and were about to break the door down. The director arrived in the nick of time with her key in hand. She unlocked the door. The first thing they checked was the sign out sheet. Had someone else picked up John? Today he went on a field trip with his class. Did he not make it back from the field trip? Was he lost somewhere? A myriad of questions ensued.

They immediately noticed that no one had signed John out. He HAD to be somewhere in the building. Everyone began a frantic search starting first with his classroom. He was not in there. Then they searched the next room and the next. John was nowhere to be found. As the police questioned the director, Mark left the daycare and began scouring the area by car.

The daycare was next to a large shopping center. Mark started his search there. Within minutes he found little John wandering around the shopping center parking lot scared, but unharmed. When he saw his daddy, he ran to him, embraced him and began to cry. He had been left alone in his classroom asleep on a mat. The daycare had shut down with him still in the room asleep. When he awoke, he had wandered to the front door of the daycare, let himself out and at 4 years old had decided he could walk home (a mere 5 miles away)!

This event started a chain of events for the family. Margaret immediately pulled John out of that daycare to put him into a private home. She vowed to find a way to make a living and also be a stay-at-home mom for her son.

Fast forward 2 years later, Margaret and Mark had a 2nd son Andrew who was now 2 years old. He also stayed with the sitter. Margaret had picked up the hobby of performing magic when John was 2 years old. She would weave magic into her sales presentations for the doctors she called on. Her innovative presentations helped her to have one of the highest market shares of any sales rep in the country and enjoy much recognition and many sales awards.

She also began to perform magic for children's birthday parties on the weekends while dressed as a clown. The weekend birthday party income was small but growing. Mark would care for the children while Margaret went out and performed at the parties. Having been deep into speech and drama in high school and public speaking while in college, it was a natural outlet for her creative side. The couple had been calculating ever since John's daycare mishap exactly how Margaret could quit her very lucrative job at Ortho Pharmaceutical and stay at home. Finally, it came to them! If Margaret could increase her weekend birthday party business, they could afford for her to quit Ortho and become a weekday stay at home Mom and a weekend party entertainer. In early July 1991 it happened. Margaret gave her boss notice. She helped hire and train her replacement. Then in August 1991, DFW Funny Business was born.

The first few years were very difficult but rewarding. Margaret performed at various children's birthday parties as Maggie the Magical Clown in the DFW area, while Mark held down the fort at home being daddy and taking care of their two growing boys.

Margaret joined several area clown clubs, took classes to hone her skills, attended state and national conventions and met and networked with other children's entertainers in the area.

Her marketing and advertising were helping her one-woman business to grow at such a pace, she found herself referring numerous parties out to other entertainers she had met through the various clubs she attended. Finally, she decided to stop referring so much work and just start acting as an entertainment agent for all these clowns while taking a commission. DFW Funny Business as an entertainment agency was born. First there were just a couple of other clowns that worked with Margaret, but later the stable of entertainers grew and grew.

Today, what was once a tiny birthday party company, is now a large corporate family entertainment agency with over 250 different entertainers. Including not only the very best clowns in the DFW area, but magicians, jugglers, stilt walkers, fire eaters, balloon artists, face painters, story tellers, DJs, caricature artists, costume characters, holiday characters, photographers, musicians, singers, puppeteers, ventriloquists, petting zoos, pony rides, kiddie trains and much more. The client list looks like a who's who in DFW including 11+ years providing Kids Zone entertainment for the Dallas Cowboys, multiple years of providing the City of Dallas special event entertainment, mall and shopping center entertainment for places like North Park Center, Watters Creek, Parks Mall, Hulen Mall, Hillside Village, Perot Companies, Great Wolf Lodge, numerous schools, churches, libraries and many more.

Her husband Mark quit the corporate life in 2010 to become the general manager for DFW Funny Business. Their son John, now an attorney, works as both a performing balloon artist, and the company's attorney. Together Mark and Margaret travel all over

Texas, Oklahoma, Arkansas and Louisiana putting smiles on children's and families faces while living the dream of owning their own entertainment business specializing in children and family entertainment.

www.dfwfunnybusiness.com

Chapter 12

<u>FUN NET™</u>

By: Clifford Todd

The FUN NET™ movement rests on love and listening while preserving the power of the network marketing business model. Love & Listen™ replace hype & greed. Using the conversational sequence Moment Time® builds quality relationships during 92% of the recommended "moments" before a FUN Netter asks for permission to talk about our services. Every moment is transformative.

In 2016, I defeated alcoholism and vowed to make network marketing fun, easy, profitable and purposeful. I took my next book to a network marketing event. The keynote speaker, Dave Blanchard, CEO of the Og Mandino Leadership Institute, read it and asked me to become one of his coaches. I started (figuratively) chasing two rabbits... teach network marketing or coach people? Three books later… I found myself still chasing two goals.

In 2018, Cancer sent me to the sidelines. A PET scan in May 2019 could not detect cancer in my body. In 2019, the U.S. Office of Patents and Trademarks registered Moment Time®. I'm now committed to transforming network marketing. Why?

People love Moment Time® for four reasons:

- No selling

- No recruiting

- No rejection

- No negative cash flow

92% of the "moments" foster heart-centered relationships with biz savvy people who check the internet before they buy. Selling disappears. That's fun and easy. People love upgrading their circles of close, loving people. Recruiting disappears. Again, fun and easy.

Sound good to you?

Once a week, and only once a week, a teammate and I talk to a person who has given me permission to talk about the transformed business model. The core questions we ask during these moments:

"If we were having this conversation a year from today, and you were looking back at the past twelve months, what would have needed to happen in your life, both personally and professionally, for you to be happy with your results?

Specifically, what dangers do you have now that need to be eliminated, what opportunities need to be captured, and what strengths need to be maximized?"

We focus on them and present FUN NET™ based on their answers. The majority join the movement. In 6-9 months, their actions blossom (> 90% do) into six-figure annual incomes. A few people go a little slower.

Your teammate is vital in these moments. If someone does not join, she or he says no to the teammate. Yes, is always said to you. Personal rejection disappears. My team and I teach people who join the movement to continue teaching everyone who joins them, until they are competent teaching those who join their teams. When teaching, people may say no, but it's never a personal rejection of the friend inviting. No time or effort is wasted.

To realistically understand the speed and power of FUN NET™, imagine you are a pro football halfback and the ball is on your goal line. It will take you 2-3 months to get to the 1-yard line. Another 2-3 months to get to the 10-yard line. During the third 2-3 months, you rocket 90 yards and score (analogously) a six-figure residual annual income.

Abundance abounds. FUN NET™ is home-based. Home-based business owners are the most tax advantaged taxpayers in America. They convert thousands of dollars of personal expenses into tax deductible business expenses and pay ZERO TAXES on the top 20% of their business net income.

Your success is bolstered by embracing these new beliefs:

OLD BELIEF	NEW BELIEF
Sell a consumable product	Choose first who you will serve.
Tell everyone about the product.	Enjoy multiple moments with few people.
Work full or part time.	80%+ listening time for < six hrs. per week.
3-5 years grinding it out.	6-9 months journeying.
99% failure rate.	Everyone coachable wins.
Sales bonuses funds effort.	Tax savings keep cash flow positive.
It's net"WORK" marketing.	Enjoy FUN NET™ love and listening.

Follow our team's guidance. I'm Clifford Todd. I know the industry.

My best 90-day check was $26,118. My highest check was $62,234. The industry's flaws are driving me to launch the FUN NET™ movement. To learn more, please request a FREE 15-minute discovery call. Email clifford@cliffordtoddbook.com. You'll be happy you did.

Thank you for being you.

Follow my guidance. My name is Clifford Todd. I'll provide details on request. You may enjoy a FREE 15-minute discovery call. Email me at <u>Clifford@Cliffordtodd.com</u> or call 513-801-1026

Chapter 13

<u>PMA During COVID-19</u>

By: Barbara Brodie

I was taught by a very intelligent man named W. Clement Stone, many years ago, who believed in the power of a positive mental attitude (PMA). Although I knew I had a strong will, and a good mental attitude, it really brought it home to me that you could control your life and your emotions.

Mr. Stone would always start his day by saying the following: I feel healthy, I feel happy, and I feel terrific. He would then ask himself, "How is my PMA?", then responding saying it was terrific. When I worked in his sales force, our team would start every morning with that mantra before we started our business. Our job was difficult. Going around selling insurance, being shown the door more times than it was open, teaches you to cope with and handle rejection. One of the ways you coped was by having a strong positive mental attitude (PMA).

Over the past fifty years, I have used PMA daily. I have been through a lot of different things during my time and the main thing I have learned is that you just have to go with the flow. You must focus on one day at a time. Many years ago, when my marriage ended, I was left with nothing while raising my son, Paul. I had no job and had to rebuild. There was no point in thinking, "Oh I had a wonderful life. I had lots of money, a beautiful home, and now I have nothing." I started over again and took one day at a time by just getting out of bed and keeping a positive mental attitude. My goal was to be kind to everyone and do the best that I could each day.

The only job I could find was as a person who stood inside the mall and asked people to take market research surveys. I was used to people saying no, so that did not bother me. Over the next few months, I became the top producer at the branch. At the time, I was making five dollars an hour, which would be around ten dollars an hour in our current economy. Within six months, I became the assistant manager and a few years later, became the branch manager. I worked for the company for sixteen years and was able to finally get that dream house, own a classic Ford Mustang, and enjoy the fruits of my labor.

There was no magic overnight solution. It was years of hard work, being positive, and taking one day at a time. I retired ten years ago, and life is good. This year has been a huge challenge with COVID-19. I saw a lot of people lose their jobs and saw many small businesses not survive, including many of my favorite restaurants.

With COVID, a lot of businesses have been hurt and a lot of companies have gone under. The best advice that I can give to those struggling, especially with mindset, is to continue to stay positive. Even in this situation.

If you have to start over or if you have to reorganize your business, then don't be afraid to embrace the opportunity. My son was still doing well with his publishing company, but he saw an opportunity to help people with creating virtual conferences. Now both the publishing and virtual summit businesses are thriving this year, even with COVID. Don't be afraid to pivot or to add additional services to your business.

Another thing I had to help Paul with was with dealing with COVID. He has always had challenges with depression over the years. His father has struggled with it as well. I told Paul that he needed to take up an exercise routine in addition to focusing on PMA every day, especially with sheltering in place during COVID. He has now exercised for over 200 consecutive days and his mental strength is stronger than ever. It is all about embracing change and opportunity, no matter the situation.

I have exercised for many years, from being a gymnast to riding a bike all the time when I was younger. Physical and mental exercise are both connected, and you must use both in your daily routine.

Consider starting your day with the following: I feel healthy, I feel happy, and I feel terrific. Then, ask how yourself how your PMA is and say it is terrific!

www.BrodieConsultingGroup.com

Chapter 14

<u>Prove Them Wrong</u>

By: Ashley Emma

"You won't sell any books with self-publishing," I've heard speakers say at conferences.

Some people still believe self-publishing doesn't make you a real author.

I proved them wrong.

I make a full-time income from my self-published Amish fiction books while being a stay-at-home-mom of my three young children.

I'm 29 years old and I'm an Amazon bestselling Amish fiction author of 22 books on Amazon. I publish a new book every few months. I also run my own publishing company, Fearless Publishing House, as well as my salon, Ashley's Salon, all from my home. I wrote my first novel when I was 12 and began self-publishing at age 16.

My Amish crime novels are set in the real Amish community of Unity, Maine, where I stayed with several Amish families as part of my research. The Amish were glad to teach me about their way of life in order to accurately portray them in my novels. I dressed like them while I was there and did everything they did—riding in buggies, making cheese, canning 100 quarts of applesauce, and going to church. Their community was so welcoming.

Undercover Amish was a finalist in the Maine Romance Writers Strut Your Stuff Competition 2015. *Amish Under Fire* was a semi-finalist in Harlequin's So You Think You Can Write Contest in 2015. This book is about human trafficking (modern-day slavery) in Maine, which is a very real danger more people need to know about.

My books and I have been featured on my local news station, which was a dream come true for me and super fun!

Filled with action, suspense, and dark topics, but also inspiring, my Amish novels are quite different than most. They star heroic young women who overcome huge obstacles such as murder, abortion, domestic violence, kidnapping, rape, bullying, stalking, human trafficking, and guilt.

I knew since I was a little kid that I wanted to be a novelist. I was homeschooled, so we really focused on reading and writing, which meant I had more time to read for fun. I completed 8 manuscripts before the age of 24 and was also offered my first book contract. I became a multi-bestselling author when I was 25. I worked hard for over 17 years to achieve this goal, and now it has really paid off.

One of the main reasons I always wanted to be an author was so I can share God's love with readers. I can reach a lot more people with books online than I can in person. With a book, you don't just tell readers about God, you show them through the story. My books all have strong themes of forgiveness and redemption. My characters overcome obstacles by seeking help from God. Because my books are Amish fiction, this is a major theme in my stories.

Readers email me sharing that after they've read my novels, they've realized God isn't some mean dictator or angry father, but that he is a loving and gentle father who loves us more than anything. That's why I write.

It took me about four years of seriously focused work to turn what used to be a hobby into a growing business that earns full-time income. Since I'm a stay-at-home mom, I work after my kids are in bed from about

8pm to midnight most nights, but it's worked so far for me. I now have a concrete plan to get to six figures annually.

These are the things that made the most impact in my author business:

- Taking several courses on self-publishing, growing an audience/email list, book marketing, etc.

- Growing my email list to 19,000+ readers using Facebook ads, Bookfunnel, and giving away 4 free eBooks on my website (my email list is by far the biggest reason why I am now making a full-time income)

- Doing TONS of Bookfunnel promotions monthly and having several free eBooks uploaded to use for giveaways (Bookfunnel is amazing for sales and growing your email list!)

- Amazon Ads

- Facebook Ads for selling books and growing my email list (my husband took a course and does my ads)

- Sticking to one genre, growing an audience in it, and writing series of novels in that genre (series sell better)

- Professional editing, formatting, covers, and good book descriptions

- Marketing and launching my books the right way

- Cross promoting with other authors (Bookfunnel and emailing other authors in my genre for featuring each other's books in our email newsletters)

- Releasing a new book every 3-6 months, especially books in series (this is HUGE because it keeps sales up)

- Selling exclusively on Amazon with KDP Select (I make most of my royalties from pages read in KDP Select)

- Using several permafree books on Amazon to attract new readers

Of course, there are so many more things that I did, but these are the most impactful.

Within the next 5-10 years I hope to retire my husband so he can stay home with the kids and home school them while I work. We have three children, and they're the biggest reason why I want to make a full-time income as an author—so I can spend more time with them.

Self-publishing is a TON of work for the first few years but pays off tremendously if you stick with it. Most people quit before they make a profit. It might take more or less time for you. If you have time to put the work in, you'll see results.

What an amazing world the internet has opened up to us. I can't imagine doing anything else!

Ashley Emma, bestselling Amish Fiction Author

Free Amish ebooks: www.ashleyemmaauthor.com

Free book marketing checklist and list of work-at-home jobs: http://ashleyemmaauthor.com/free-fearless-author-and-legit-work-at-home-jobs-checklist/

Amishbookwriter@gmail.com

Chapter 15

Reduce Overwhelm and Supercharge Your Results

By: Karen Ferreira

One of the most important lessons I've learned in order to achieve success and overcome overwhelm is to choose one market, sell them one product, in one way, promoted on one channel.

That's not to say you can only do this "one, one, one, one" forever. The secret is to complete this course of action to a level of success and autonomy before starting something new. Give it at least a year for development and optimization. Don't be too eager to have several pots on the fire. I can tell you, selling successfully to one market is immeasurably better than failing to sell to ten markets at the same time!

Imagine writing an email, while exercising, and reading an article, at the same as speaking to someone on the phone...all while bathing a baby. Crazy, right? Well, many of us do that in our business.

The Pareto Principle states that 80% of desired results are achieved from 20% of causes. Stated differently, most of what you want will come from the minority of your actions. Doing only one thing may take this to the extreme, but it will get you better results than doing ten things. Narrowing your focus directly impacts your level of success.

Many of us know this data in some form but knowing and doing are not the same thing.

You may feel if you only choose one market or product, you'll miss out on so many untapped possibilities. Yes, it's scary to "niche down until it hurts", or to even abandon certain things you've already started, but it's worth it.

Staying one course makes it possible for "failures" to become learning experiences. If you change course each time you "fail", how will you ever improve? To become great at anything, it takes learning and doing repeatedly. No painter became great by painting once and saying, "This isn't the result I wanted, let me try a different medium." No, they painted again and again and again, each time with the same kind of paint.

So, ready to cut back, simplify, and succeed like never before?

I'm all about action steps, so here are some bird's-eye view steps to get you started. Bonus points if you do them right now.

1. If you don't have a market yet, choose one. If you have more than one market, choose one. Who will you serve? The market you choose is important. If you're not sure how to choose the right one, I recommend reading Choose by Ryan Levesque.

2. Now do the same for your product or service. What does your market need or desire? Research it by seeing what people are spending money on. If you don't have a product or service, or have more than one, choose only one. It can be low-ticket, high-ticket, or somewhere in-between.

3. Decide how you will sell your product. Again, choose one way, for example:

   - a webinar (live or evergreen)

   - a free plus shipping funnel (sending potential customers a free book or product and they only cover shipping)

   - a quiz funnel

- a video sales letter

- talking to them on the phone or in person

4. How will you reach your target audience? You could use paid ads on one chosen platform (Facebook, Google, YouTube or others), leverage the email lists of others, use your own email list if you have one, etc. Again, pick one.

5. Create a plan to execute the above steps. This includes learning skills needed, hiring the right people to help you on certain steps, and listing out each action needed. A plan enables you to prioritize the actions that will get actual results. It reduces overwhelm and keeps reorienting you to your purpose. Purpose determines priority. Priority determines our actions and how productive these actions are. A plan is only valuable if it gets executed. You need daily action to stick to it.

6. First, determine your goals for the next twelve weeks. Then break down your list of all the needed actions into monthly, then weekly, steps for the next twelve weeks. List everything you intend to achieve for each week.

7. Each day write a to-do list based on your plan. If anything, you put on the list   doesn't directly relate to your one market, product, funnel or reach method, remove it from the list. Successful people work based on pre-defined priorities. Write your to-do list with results in mind.

If everything on your daily list falls within your chosen path, but there is too much to do, circle the two to three most important tasks—the ones that will move you towards your goal the fastest—and do those.

It's easy to get caught up in emails and lots of tasks that "need" to get done. We tend to fill our days with busy work, but how much of what we do moves the needle towards achieving our goals? I know I have spent many days working hard, only to look back and realized I hadn't moved one iota closer to my goal. Yes, life will still happen. Things pop up, and you can't stop answering emails altogether.

It's crucial to schedule time daily to execute your strategic plan, and guard that time. Working on only one strategy has the major benefit of helping you to stay focused. It empowers you to stick to a course of action and not get sucked into meaningless or low-reward activities.

Choosing all your "ones" and then laying out a clear strategy and sticking to it will change the way you operate, and in short order it will noticeably boost your levels of success, guaranteed.

www.childrensbookmastery.com

Chapter 16

<u>The Best $100 I've Ever Spent: From Elephant Dung to CEO</u>

By: Qat Wanders

Standing next to a circus tent in Southern India, with mud and elephant dung up to my mid-calves, I moved to swat yet another gargantuan mosquito away from my face. It was 6 AM and already over one hundred degrees Fahrenheit. It had rained all night long, so the humidity made the air thick enough to practically chew rather than breathe.

It was my turn to get the elephants ready for the show that day. As much as I enjoyed bonding with the magnificent creatures, it was exhausting work.

Traveling with the circus had been a cool job when I was in my early twenties, but when I hit thirty, it stopped being so glamorous. My body felt worn and I was dealing with severe chronic pain, which made everything even more difficult.

On top of all this, I had been struggling to get custody of my daughter, but my constant traveling made it nearly impossible.

Bzzzt.

Smack.

Another mosquito bit me on my throat. I wiped away the blood-filled insect looking at what was left of it on my hand in disgust...

"I'm not doing this anymore!" I said out loud...

Even though the only ones around to hear me were the elephants, that was my declaration to the universe. I had made up my mind.

There *had* to be something else I could do. But what was I supposed to put on my resume? "Traveling circus performer with ten years of elephant-care experience"? I mean, I could probably become a Starbucks barista or something, right?

Truth be told, I had gathered plenty of life and job experience over the years, but it was obscure and I didn't think any of it would help with getting a new job. I was a certified yoga therapist and licensed skydiver, I had trained and been certified in functional medicine and Ayurveda, and I did freelance writing and editing gigs on the side while I traveled the world. I held a BA and MA in English and Editing and had worked in traditional publishing in my younger years. That was before I decided the career was too stuffy for me and ran away with the circus... Literally.

Okay, so I had skills. Now what?

I made my way back to the United States and moved in with a couple friends in Colorado. I had no family or support system, but I had saved up a little bit of money in my travels to cover my food and rent for several months, plus a little extra to purchase a Chromebook and a $100 online course claiming to teach me to *kickstart* my own freelance business.

It turned out to be the best $100 I've ever spent in my life.

I followed the course exactly: picked a business name, got an EIN, set up a business account... then I *hustled.* I used my experience with traditional publishing and the English language as leverage to get immediate freelance writing and editing jobs and started to build an even bigger client base.

And I networked, networked, networked.

Less than a year later, I had moved into my own three-story house in the suburbs with my daughter.

That little writing/editing business, Wandering Words Media, went from zero to six figures in less than a year, then grew to seven figures within three years. Now I'm the CEO with a full team of stellar writers and editors.

Was it easy? No. Was I just lucky? No. Do I have a magic strategy to share? No. I worked my ass off. And then I worked some more.

It all started with that $100 course that gave me the inspiration to know it was possible. Add to that the grit and determination I developed throughout years of travel in harsh conditions. Then I just set my mind on my goal and never gave up!

I continued to sign up for dozens of other courses and always had a mentor to help me fine tune my business.

It worked for me because I *decided* it would. I did a lot of things right, but I also screwed a lot of stuff up in the process.

My biggest takeaway through all this? Things don't always fall into place the way we want them to, but if we can adapt and keep going, they eventually fall into place the way we need them to.

www.wanderingwordsmedia.com

Chapter 17

Thriving During Covid-19

By: Alinka Rutkowska

There are two types of businesses: those set up to suffer during Covid and those set up to thrive.

If you're a restaurant, you're obviously set up to suffer, if not die. Unless you turn your restaurant into a grocery store, which has to remain open.

But if you're a travel guide and borders are closed or people are locked down, then obviously the pandemic won't be your best time in terms of revenue generation.

You need to pivot and go online.

Then, there are businesses that are set up to thrive. Pretty much everything & anything online, like businesses helping people set up an online business, or others like my publishing company, Leaders Press.

We're actually benefiting from everything shifting online. Last year an office in New York might have been considered the ultimate display of prestige. Now it's torture. Last year people liked to do business face to face, now they're afraid to get out of the house.

Due to the pandemic, our way of doing business is not considered an alternative anymore. It has become the only viable way.

Instead of shrinking and closing down like many, we're exploding with new clients, new projects, and new services.

But it's not only luck.

There's mindset here too.

I did not decrease my prices and I do not work for free. Through my mastermind groups, I've learned early on that if you start thinking recessionary, you start acting recessionary, and you slowly kill your business.

Instead of shifting our thinking, we doubled our marketing and we're hiring like never before. We even came up with a new service that is selling like gangbusters.

So, what you do if you're a traditional offline business? The only survival strategy, whether in a pandemic or not, is to adapt.

I live in a beautiful little village by the sea and we had a very strict lockdown. One of the first businesses to re-open was a local pizza place that at first only re-opened their home delivery operation. When I called to order at 7:00 pm, they said they had so many orders they could deliver the pizza at 10:00 pm. They managed to regroup and grab the lion's share of the market.

If you're in the physical events business, this probably isn't your best year either. Meeting people in person and mingling with a cocktail is amazing, but you can offer the next best thing - an online event. There's technology for it! I recently participated in a 300-person live zoom meeting (btw, if you're Zoom, you're winning), you can still do break-out sessions. Bonus - I no longer have to fly and beat jet lag to benefit from this!

I'm sure there are many scenarios and circumstances and people not having the best time of their lives, but you can always adapt. If you're part of a house keeping team in a hotel and the hotel closes down for the season, how about going online and regrouping as a Virtual Assistant or a transcriptionist?

We are programmed to be shocked by change, but often, it can be a blessing in disguise.

Go to www.leaderspress.com/book to get a free copy of "Outsource Your Book" (ebook and audio book!).

Go to www.authorremake.com/book to get a free copy of my award-winning guide "How I Sold 80,000 Books".

Chapter 18

<u>Proud to be a Rotarian</u>

By: Paul Brodie

In 2018, when I decided to get more involved in my local community, I was faced with a choice.

Do I join a Rotary Club or my local Chamber of Commerce?

Initially, I joined the Greater Arlington Chamber of Commerce and a funny thing happened. Many of the business owners in the Chamber were also in Rotary. I thought that maybe I could do both.

One of the business owners invited my friends and me to check out the Arlington Sunrise Rotary Club. The club met every Friday morning and started at 7:00 am sharp. We could not believe what an energetic club they were. You would never know it was that early in the morning.

They were a great group of people ranging in age from the mid-twenties to the eighties. I feel that one of the misconceptions about Rotary is that it consists of mainly older people. While there are a lot of older members, there are also many Rotarians in their twenties, thirties, and forties as there are many ways to be involved in Rotary. There are eight different type of club models ranging from traditional clubs to E-Clubs (virtual only), and many other options.

In April 2019, I went to Maui and I wanted to see how Rotary was done outside my area. I attended the Rotary Club of Kihei-Wailea meeting while in Maui and that was when I became a Rotarian. Becoming a

Rotarian is when you see the true impact of Rotary on a worldwide scale. Many people see the impact quickly while others may take years to see it. There were over thirty people at the meeting and eight of the people were guests from Rotary Clubs from across the world. I contacted the club president prior to the trip to ask if we would do a club banner exchange. During the meeting, we had a quick exchange ceremony as we traded our respective club banners. It was an amazing experience and showed me the world impact of community that Rotary has.

During this time, my publishing business was growing quickly, and it was becoming difficult to be able to attend those early Friday Rotary Club meetings. After much consideration, I transferred to the Rotary Club of Arlington Highlands. My good friends, Ruben and Bryan were my first recruits and came along with me. We were all installed together in June 2019.

This club was different. They had a lot of growing pains as they were chartered in 2016 and were still figuring things out. There was a lot of turnover and I knew that if I did not step up into a leadership position, then the club may not continue. I started with recruiting speakers for the club and was able to bring in multiple business leaders to talk including the Mayor of Arlington and the CEO of the Greater Chamber of Commerce. I also took over as Treasurer since the previous one left the club. My mentality was to take the bull by the horns and take recruitment on for our club with Co-Chairing the Director of Membership position.

From 2019 to September 2020, I recruited eight new members, which accounted for 80 percent of our current membership. Our club is now thriving as every club has their own personality and culture. I mention this because every club is different. In some situations, you can just be a member and in others you may have to step up to help the club improve and grow. In January 2020, I was elected as the President-Elect for the Rotary Club of Arlington Highlands and look forward to serving as President in 2021 when the Rotary fiscal year begins.

Our club meets twice a month: on a Tuesday evening at 6:30 pm, which was perfect for our schedules. With COVID-19 we are meeting virtually and hope to adopt a hybrid model in the future for meetings. Even during COVID, we recruited multiple members so it shows that you can build momentum even in these circumstances.

Rotary was founded in 1905 by Chicago attorney, Paul Harris and there are over 1.2 million people in the Rotary Network. The two main mottos of Rotary are Service Above Self and One Profits Most Who Serves Best. Rotary has many wonderful service projects with the main priority to eradicate polio. In 1985, Rotary launched PolioPlus and was a founding member of the Global Polio Eradication Initiative in 1988. Through these efforts, over 2.5 billion have received the polio vaccine.

The main thing I love about Rotary is the opportunity to serve our local, national, and international community.

If you are interested in becoming a member then please feel free to reach out as the world can always use more Rotarians.

Proud to be a Rotarian!

https://portal.clubrunner.ca/12907

Chapter 19

<u>Serve No Master</u>

By: Jonathan Green

On Friday, February 10, 2010, I signed a six-month lease on a new apartment with a friend of mine. On Saturday, I signed a five-year loan on a new convertible. On Monday, there was a blizzard and I drove my new convertible into work. As I walked through the door, I was fired.

My world instantly came crashing down.

I was slipping and sliding on my way home. I only had two thoughts in my head - number one, please do not let me get in a car accident on the way home from being fired. And number two, I never want someone to have this level of power over me again. Over the next six months, I dedicated myself to building a new career where no one would have the ability to take away my livelihood. Because when you lose your job, you lose your income, your home, your transportation, and your food.

I realized that my boss had far too much power over me and the ability to affect my life and there was nothing I could do about it.

I began my journey by buying an expensive course that I couldn't afford, with six monthly payments, maxing out my credit card. And every month I worked so hard to make enough money to hit that payment. I never even considered stopping the payments or canceling the credit card because the boats had burned behind me. I never wanted to go back to work again. I dedicated myself to working harder and harder and putting in 14-hour days, 18-hour days, whatever it took to build a business. My dedication slowly began to pay off as I met more and more people who wanted to work on projects with me. I found mentors and success.

The lesson that I learned along this journey was that the only thing you need to succeed is motivation. It's amazing to me how many people I meet who bought the exact same course I started with, watch the first video, quit, never took action, and then complain that the course didn't work. Now there are other people that were going through the exact same course they were always on the weekly video showing how much money they were making, and there are people making far more money than me, massively outperforming me. That just motivated me to work harder and harder to transform my life.

Over the past 10 years, I've gone from losing that apartment and moving back into my mother's basement to traveling the world and living on a tropical island and starting an amazing family.

10 years ago, I never would have thought that losing my job would be the best thing that ever happened to me. It turns out it was because I never would have found that motivation to take control of my destiny. If they hadn't fired me, I might still be working. They're making less than I play my employees who work for me right now. Along the way, I've written hundreds of books, created dozens of products and worked with some amazing people across the spectrum of business.

At every step of the way, the journey has been challenging, but wonderful. It's scary to be in charge of your own destiny. And that's what causes so many of us to hold back. We're so afraid of taking action, but when you do, you begin to realize that greatness is within you and you're capable of so much more than you ever thought was possible. For so long, I thought I wasn't smart enough or good enough at math. I thought I didn't have what it takes to be an entrepreneur. As it turns out, all of those thoughts were dead wrong.

If you believe in yourself, if you make a commitment, and if you put in the time, you can succeed. The secret to success and building a business is not about being an outlier or superstar. It's about playing Moneyball, which means putting in consistent action every day. There are so many people that are better writers than me, more eloquent, more emotional masters and have the metaphor – yet they're still struggling to make ends meet.

Because while they have flashes of inspiration, every single day, I put in the same hours of work, work my way through my task list and prepare for the next day's tasks. It's that consistent daily action that generates success rather than short, sprints in business. Life is a marathon. If you commit to putting in one to three hours a day, every single day, as long as you don't quit and as long as you stick to a single business plan that works, success becomes inevitable.

Serve no master.

jonathan@servenomaster.com

Chapter 20

<u>The Art of Not Giving Up</u>

By: Ray Brehm

I was about to give up.

That idea made me feel sad, nauseated, and downright depressed.

The dream business I had envisioned for so long was not providing the income I needed to sustain it, let alone my family.

I wasn't sure where I was going to go next, and it wasn't a good feeling at all.

Now, I had been laid off and jobless before, but this time it was different.

I was now on my own, living my dream...except I wasn't making a consistent income.

I had done everything right, or so I thought.

Creativity, technology, and connections were my passion. Friendships and family were my measurement of wealth. I still needed some type of consistent income.

The lure of being a bestselling author is that it is the path to financial independence. And don't get me wrong, being called a bestselling author is cool and creates authority, but a book alone will not be your breadwinner. I had learned that a few years earlier.

Yet, by word of mouth, I had built a business around helping others launch their books to bestsellers.

It was then I ran into the same issue. Vanity and authority will not pay the bills alone. Even as I was getting paid to help others launch their books, the same phrase kept coming back.

Books are not your breadwinner. They are valuable in creating authority, increasing sales and marketing, but when you try to use them as your sole source of income, you are in for a rude awakening.

I had tried to make them the breadwinner for me, that didn't work.

I then tried launching books for others, it was not the right fit.

In order for me to serve my clients, I always let them know that the myth about royalties creating a passive income was few and far between.

There was something missing. The ability to help my clients create that missing income they thought would come from books.

As I struggled through my financial situation, I had scheduled to host my own virtual summit.

During the process, I made many great connections with other leaders in different fields. In fact, I discovered that is quite easy to do when you are asking others to be interviewed on a summit.

When my summit started, surprisingly money started to flow in. My email list grew, and my authority increased.

It was then I realized what I was meant to do. I was meant to help authors realize the role of their books, and to help them make money from virtual summits.

I partnered with my friend Paul Brodie on the next step in my journey, Done-For-You virtual summits for authors and entrepreneurs.

All of this would have been for nothing, had I not pushed through that initial down spell. I would never have discovered the power of virtual summits to build email lists, make connections with influencers, and create income.

I would not have learned the subtle art of not giving up.

www.VirtualSummitSystem.com

Chapter 21

Invest in Yourself

By: Michelle Hacker

"There is a difference between poor and broke. Broke is temporary. Poor is eternal." -Robert T. Kiyosaki

Growing up on the Southside of Chicago I saw plenty of blue-collar workers and workers lower than blue collar. People selling anything, holding any sign for any business, or selling roses on the street to make quick cash. My father didn't get up every morning and put on a crisply starched shirt and complimenting tie, then look for his briefcase to rush out the door… There was no eagerly waiting for his vacation time so we could go on a family vacation, every year. And business? Well, let's just say that the business world was something we only saw on TV while rooting for the female climbing that ladder. It was this life that shaped my view of business, the working world, and my own goals.

Becoming a teen mother changed my entire view on life. This meant, I knew that I had to work harder, longer, and attain an education if I was to have any chance of success in the name of financial security. I not only had to navigate my way alone, but with two children in tow. For those of you who may not know, it's hard trying to work to support two kids, when you have two kids. Everyone wants to babysit that first baby, the one everyone has been waiting for, but tell them there are two and you find yourself on the short list of people to avoid.

One day my unmotivated ex-boyfriend gave me a book titled, "Rich Dad, Poor Dad" by Robert T. Kiyosaki. The book had been given to him as a gift, a motivational tool, if you will. Purchased by his friend to try to get him to use his natural talents to become one of the elites. That still makes me laugh.

I was in my last semester of college when I finally read the book. It still completely baffles me how I couldn't bring my youthful head, full of healthy brains, to understand the concept "pay yourself first." This book explains that the idea behind paying yourself even before you pay your electric bill, is how you begin the road toward independent wealth. I can still feel my eyeroll. As I continued to read, what I'm digesting is lessons that I now know to be true.

1. Some people get angry at life pushing them around, and knowing no better, they push back, but at everyone and everything except life – *The meaning here is not to waste time fighting against things, people, who have no control over your own life.*

2. Life pushes all of us around, some people give up and some people fight – *If you learn this lesson early in life you will grow to be wealthy and wise at a younger age than most. Who doesn't agree as this as the ultimate life goal?*

3. If you don't learn this lesson you will spend the rest of your life waiting/expecting for some big break that will solve all of your financial problems – *Hm.*

4. Most people will spend their entire lives working for money instead of making money work for them – *Change your point of view!*

I wish I knew then how simply a philosophy can change your entire world…in your favor!

As I got older, I realized that the only things that are a "big deal" are those things you give validation to. Finding meaning or importance in things good and bad, positive and negative, gives those things power over you. It is only when you put yourself on a pedestal can you see what needs to be changed to ensure true happiness. Instead of blaming yourself or others, fix it. It really is that simple. Don't stay angry, you are only wasting your time. Give yourself a salary, pay yourself first. Everyone else can wait. I understand that people might wonder how a single mother chooses to pay herself over the electric company in the winter, I truly do. But think of it like this;

You know you will always find a way to keep those lights on. You will beg, borrow, or steal to get what you need for your family. Likewise, what the smoker spends is often looked back on with astonishment. Had you paid yourself before that tobacco company and the taxes, you would be the one sitting high on the hog. The point is, we find excuses if that's what we want. True, some people may not know that they are looking for excuses, and some people are just afraid of change. One thing is sure, while I have no regrets in life, I wish I would've learned to put myself first when I was young.

It is said that you will always find a way; you will find a way to get cigarettes, pay the electric bill, and a million other things that will do nothing for ourselves or our future. Find a way to give yourself the life you want as early as you can, find excuses TO PAY YOURSELF FIRST. You are your greatest investment.

wutusaygoes@gmail.com

Chapter 22

<u>"Welcome to the Family"</u>

By: Cindy & John Salter

What comes to mind when you hear "family business"? A father-son or perhaps husband-wife team running a small, local shop?

Ours is a family business. What does that mean to be part of the Salter Bros. Coffee Roasters family? It's more than you might think.

As a husband and wife team who founded our specialty coffee roasting company in our hometown of Arlington, Texas, it's obvious that we're a family business. Our children help with the business, each plugging in where their natural talents align with company needs. Our oldest son, gifted with an analytical mind, does our finances. Our other son, a forestry student who thrives on working with his hands, is a roaster. Lastly, our daughter, a business school major, provides marketing input and attends networking events with us. Like in any family, everyone has unique talents, with each member tied together with a common thread.

Our family certainly has a genuine love for good coffee. To us, coffee is part of our family, and has been for much of our lives. Even the smell of coffee can stir childhood memories of enjoying a cup with beloved family members (some of whom now live on only in our hearts), often after a special family meal or holiday celebration.

When we launched our roasting business, we really only intended to offer custom roasted coffee for our customers to brew and enjoy at home, in their workplace, or at the restaurants and cafes who serve our coffee. That was the plan. As we began meeting with more people, many asked if we planned to open a place for them to come in and sit down over a cup of coffee. They were asking about a local, neighborhood coffeehouse run by an independent coffee roaster. Thus, our business family expanded, so to speak, and we've opened the Salter Bros. Coffeehouse & Roastery, situated in the heart of downtown, where we roast coffee and also serve it. Our family began to grow.

As with many families, sometimes you evolve in unexpected and wonderful ways, responding to needs and the desire for a sense of belonging and connectedness. That's how we view our decision to open our coffeehouse. When we roast and serve you coffee, we consider you part of our family, for it's a sense of hospitality and service that we feel is a cornerstone of what we do.

Let's take a closer look at the coffee we've chosen to import, roast, and serve, and we hope you'll appreciate another facet of our "family coffee business" that may not have been as obvious. We decided from the start to roast exclusively *specialty coffee*. That means that rather than buy bulk coffee beans as a commodity, we research and work closely with our certified coffee importers to learn about each country and its regions, lots, and farms, and learn about the people who actually grow the coffee. Think about it— someone planted, cultivated, and harvested these coffee beans, nurturing the soil and growing conditions to bring out nuances in flavor and unique characteristics of each region's offerings. Often, it's generations of family growers, or a community of families working together to produce the best crops, whose coffee we select. That's the coffee that we roast and serve you. It's the family story behind each cup. It's very special coffee, grown by special people, for very special people.

So, when we say, "Welcome to the family", it's a community that spans the globe, connected by a desire to enjoy and savor, some really good, really special coffee.

We're Salter Bros. Coffee Roasters, and we invite you to be part of our family.

www.SalterBrosCoffee.com

Coffeehouse & Roastery

400 E. Division St.

Arlington, Texas 76011

<u>Strategy Session Invitation</u>

Hope that you have enjoyed reading our business book.

This was truly a labor of love and it was an honor to help these 75 amazing people share their story.

If you would like to discuss your potential book, then we would love to talk with you.

In celebration of our business book, I would like to extend a personal invitation to you for a complimentary strategy session.

It is a no-pitch session and all we want to do is to find out more about you and your potential book to see if we can help.

This is not a sales call.

Our only intention is to see if and how we can help you.

Due to time constraints, the call must be limited to 15-minutes. Are you ready to get started?

- Go to -
<u>www.GetPublishedSystem.com</u>
and click on the Complimentary Strategy Session tab

Contact Information

Paul can be reached at **Brodie@BrodieConsultingGroup.com**

Website **www.GetPublishedSystem.com**

Publishing and Coaching Services

www.GetPublishedSystem.com/services

Speaking and Keynotes **http://www.BrodieEDU.com/seminars**

Get Published Podcast **www.GetPublishedPodcast.com**

Join our Get Published Facebook Group by typing **Get Published**

in the Facebook search bar

Follow Paul on Instagram **www.instagram.com/paulgbrodie**

Follow Paul on Twitter **www.twitter.com/Get   Published**

Like Paul's Author Page on **www.facebook.com/paulgbrodieauthor/**

Connect with Paul on LinkedIn **www.linkedin.com/in/paulgbrodie**

Feedback Request

Please leave a review for our book as I would greatly appreciate your feedback.

If for some reason you did not enjoy the book then please contact me at **Brodie@BrodieConsultingGroup.com** to discuss options prior to leaving a negative review and please feel free to let me know how the book can be improved.